101 THINGS EVERY KID NEEDS TO KNOW

Important Skills That Prepare Kids for Life!

CONTENTS

Be Yourself & People Skills

Chapter 1 — Make Friends

Friendship begins with small, brave acts that tell other people you are safe to approach. Smile, offer your name, and ask a simple, genuine question that opens a doorway—how their project is going, what they like to read, whether they've tried the new game at recess. Notice who looks open to conversation: eyes up, relaxed shoulders, a curious glance back at you. Keep early chats balanced so you talk and listen in roughly equal amounts. Share a little about yourself, not everything at once, and follow up the next day with a warm hello so the connection does not fade.

Over time, trust grows from consistency and kindness. Remember names and one small detail, then bring it up later to show you were paying attention. Offer small help without expecting payback, and accept "no" with grace so people feel safe around you. If someone seems shy or unsure, lower the pressure by inviting them into low-stakes moments—sitting together, practicing together, or joining your group for a short task. You do not need to be loud or wildly funny; you need to be steady, respectful, and willing to try again. That steady courage turns classmates into real friends.

Chapter 2 — Be a Good Friend

Being a good friend means being reliable, caring, and honest in ways that match what your friend needs. Show up when you said you would, even for small plans, because reliability is the quiet glue of friendship. Listen without rushing to fix every problem; often people want to feel understood more than they want a solution. Keep promises and safe secrets, and if you cannot keep a promise, tell the truth early with kindness. Check in after big days like games, tests, and concerts—your attention says, “You matter to me,” which is the best gift friends can give.

Good friends celebrate wins without envy and offer comfort without drama. When a friend succeeds, congratulate them and notice the specific efforts behind the result; when they struggle, sit close to the feeling rather than trying to make it disappear. Healthy friendships also include boundaries: you can say no without guilt, and you can accept no without pushing. Repair mistakes with real apologies and patient actions. Over months and years, those simple habits create friendships that can carry both laughter and storms.

Chapter 3 — Everyday Manners

Manners are small habits that help people feel respected and comfortable around you, and they make the world move more smoothly. Speak with a friendly tone, use names correctly, and say "please," "thank you," and "excuse me" as part of your normal day. Give people your eyes when they're talking and put devices away so your attention says, "I'm here." Match your volume to the place—soft in libraries, lively but not loud at games. Hold doors, share space, and tidy common areas without being asked because shared spaces belong to all of us.

At the table, use napkins rather than sleeves and chew with your mouth closed. If you bump someone, apologize even if it was an accident. Let others finish their sentences, then answer in one clear thought rather than three. When you make a mistake, a brief honest apology is stronger than an excuse. Manners are not fancy rules to impress strangers; they are everyday signals of care for the people nearby. Practiced steadily, they turn ordinary moments—classrooms, buses, family meals—into places where everyone can breathe a little easier.

Chapter 4 — Listen Like a Pro

Listening well is not passive; it is an active skill that earns trust. Face the speaker with your eyes and body, quiet your hands, and let your attention land fully on their words. Instead of planning your reply while they are still speaking, focus on the last sentence they said so you catch the point that matters most. Short echoes—"So you tried the new drill"—and one clear question show you are following the path of their thoughts. When they pause, resist the urge to fill the silence; thoughtful pauses help people find better words.

Great listeners notice feelings as well as facts. They hear the excitement hidden in a quick story, or the worry hiding underneath a joke, and they respond with empathy rather than judgment. Taking simple notes in class or during team huddles keeps details from slipping away later. At the end of a conversation, a one-sentence summary and a next step—"So we meet at three to finish slides"—turns talk into action. Listening like this makes people want to include you, and it makes you learn faster, because what you understand the first time, you do not need to relearn later.

Chapter 5 — Speak Up Confidently

Confident speaking is a practice, not a personality. Begin by standing tall and taking one slow breath to steady your pace. Lead with your main point in one clear sentence, then offer a couple of short reasons or examples to anchor it. Use everyday words and strong verbs so your ideas land cleanly. When you feel rushy, pause at natural breaks; silence is a tool, not a failure. If a thought wanders, gently return to your point and close with a simple request or next step so listeners know what to do.

You grow faster by listening to yourself. Practice out loud, record thirty seconds, and review what worked: your speed, clarity, and eye contact. Replace filler phrases with brief pauses. Ask one question that draws others in—"What do you think about trying it on Friday?"—so speaking becomes a conversation, not a performance. Confidence is not being the loudest voice; it is telling the truth clearly and kindly. Every time you speak up with calm accuracy, your confidence grows another quiet inch.

Chapter 6 — Handle Bullying

Bullying is repeated, hurtful behavior that involves a power imbalance, and everyone deserves to feel safe from it. If someone targets you, keep your posture tall and your voice firm as you state a clear boundary—"Stop. That's not okay"—then move toward safer people and places. Record details such as who was involved, what happened, and where and when it occurred. Tell a trusted adult promptly, and keep telling until action is taken. Offline or online, your job is not to win an argument; your job is to protect your safety and dignity and to bring the right helpers into the situation.

Strength grows when communities act together. Walk with a buddy in risky areas and be the kind of bystander who notices, interrupts safely, and reports. Online, block and report, save evidence, and step away from screens to give your nervous system a break. None of this is your fault, and you are not weak for asking for help; you are wise. When you support others who are targeted, you help build a culture where meanness loses its audience and kindness keeps its ground.

Chapter 7 — Boundaries & Consent

Boundaries are the lines that protect your comfort, time, and safety; consent is clear permission freely given. The first skill is noticing your own signals—tight shoulders, a knot in your stomach, a thought that says, "I don't want this." Put those signals into words early and simply: "No, thanks," "Please stop," or "I'm not comfortable with that." Ask before touching or borrowing, and accept no immediately without testing the boundary or pushing for a different answer. Clear speech protects both people and relationships because it removes guessing games.

Healthy boundaries are not walls; they are doors with good hinges. Share your preferences in everyday moments—how you like to be greeted, what kinds of jokes feel okay, how much advance notice you need before plans. Respecting others' limits shows maturity; when someone sets a boundary with you, thank them for being clear. If a person repeatedly ignores your limits, seek help from adults who can intervene. The more you practice asking, listening, and accepting answers, the more your friendships and teams will feel safe and strong.

Chapter 8 — Apologize & Forgive

A good apology repairs trust. Name what you did without excuses, acknowledge the impact, and say you are sorry in a tone that matches your words. Offer a concrete way to make it right or to prevent the harm next time. Then give the other person time; forgiveness cannot be demanded. If you are the person forgiving, you are choosing to release the hold the hurt has on your energy. You can forgive and still remember the lesson, and you can forgive without keeping a situation the same.

Apologies are strongest when they are brief, honest, and followed by changed behavior. "I'm sorry, but…" weakens responsibility by shifting blame. Long explanations look like defenses; truth needs fewer words. If you are not ready to apologize because you are still heated, pause until you can speak calmly. Friendships grow when both people learn to repair conflict wisely.

Chapter 9 — Share & Take Turns

Sharing and taking turns turn competition into cooperation. Before a game or activity, agree on what fairness will look like: time limits, a number of turns, or a rotation of roles so everyone gets to try something new. Use a timer everyone can see so the rule manages the moment, not one person's mood. Thank others for their turn, and keep shared spaces tidy so the next person starts fresh rather than cleaning up your mess. When disagreements appear, pause, restate the rule, and begin again.

Practicing fairness builds muscles you will use for the rest of life. Offer choices that still feel fair—"You pick first this time, I'll pick first next time"—so people feel respected rather than controlled. Celebrate good play more than winning. When you notice yourself wanting to grab and keep, try trading the desire to own for the chance to enjoy together. The habit of sharing does not make things less special; it makes people more connected, and that is a win that lasts longer than any single turn.

Chapter 10 — Include Others

Inclusion is the daily work of making space where people feel they belong. Start by noticing who is on the edge and invite them into low-pressure moments: a seat at your table, a role during group work, a chance to share ideas. Use names and eye contact to show real welcome. Avoid inside jokes that shut people out, and create simple team rules that give different kinds of strengths a chance to shine. When a plan unintentionally excludes someone, change the plan rather than the person.

Belonging does not require pretending everyone is the same; it requires honoring differences and giving access to what matters. Ask people what would help them participate more fully, then follow through. Speak to people directly rather than about them, and check your assumptions about what someone can or cannot do. Inclusion is not extra work tacked onto the side of life; it is the way we build classrooms, clubs, and communities where more people get to contribute. The best teams are the ones where nobody has to earn their seat at the table.

Chapter 11 — Teamwork

Teams succeed when goals are shared, roles are clear, and people treat one another with respect. Begin by naming the goal in one sentence so everyone can point their effort in the same direction. Decide who will do what and by when, then check progress at regular moments rather than waiting until the deadline. Keep feedback specific and kind so ideas improve without making people feel small. Write decisions down so the team does not lose time debating the same thing again next week.

Great teams match tasks to strengths and still help members grow new skills. They share credit widely and own mistakes together. When friction appears, return to the shared goal and ask what option best serves it. Celebrate results and also talk about what you learned on the way, because process lessons make future projects smoother. Teamwork is not one person doing everything and others watching; it is the art of many hands building one thing well.

Chapter 12 — Solve Conflicts

Conflicts are normal whenever people care about the same things and see different paths. Start by pausing long enough to cool down so you can speak without attacking. Explain your view using “I” statements that name what you saw, how you felt, and what you need now. Ask to hear the other person fully and listen without interrupting; often you will discover a shared goal underneath the tension. Then look for options that meet both sets of needs, even if neither side gets one hundred percent of what they wanted.

Staying on today's issue prevents old arguments from taking over. If you get stuck, invite a neutral helper to guide the conversation toward an agreement you can both accept. Write down the agreement in one sentence and decide how you will check whether it's working. Conflict is not a sign that a friendship or team is broken; it is a chance to practice courage, clarity, and care. Every fair solution you reach together strengthens trust.

Learn Smarter

Chapter 13 — Growth Mindset

A growth mindset is the belief that abilities can be developed through effort, strategies, and help. It turns “I can’t” into “I can’t yet.” When you face a tough skill, notice where you improved last time, choose a strategy to test next, and track the minutes you practiced rather than only the result. Compare yourself to your past self, not to the best person in the room.

Mistakes become useful when you treat them like information. After a try, ask what worked, what didn’t, and what you will do differently. Celebrate progress in small steps: clearer handwriting, one more correct answer, a smoother passage in music. Avoid fixed labels like “not a math person” or “bad at sports”; they close doors your future self may want to walk through.

Chapter 14 — Focus & Attention

Attention is your brain's spotlight; where you point it, you learn. Clear your space so only needed items are within reach, and put devices out of sight so they stop whispering for your focus. Set a short work interval and begin with the hardest step while your energy is fresh. When stray thoughts pop up, jot them on a "parking" note and return to the task. After a focused stretch, stand, sip water, and breathe; breaks help attention last longer.

Single-tasking beats multitasking because switching costs time and energy. If you struggle to start, apply the two-minute rule: begin any tiny piece that takes less than two minutes, and momentum will carry you forward. Choose background noise that supports your brain—quiet for some, gentle hum for others—and reserve small treats for study time so your mind links effort with pleasure. Attention grows with routines, just like muscles grow with workouts. Treat it kindly, and it will carry you far.

Chapter 15 — Time Management Basics

Time management is the art of choosing what matters first and finishing on time without rushing at the end. Start the day by naming a small list of important tasks and estimating how many minutes each will take. Break big assignments into steps that begin with verbs—write the outline, solve five problems, review pages one to three—so you know exactly how to start. Give yourself a start time, not just a deadline, and protect it like an appointment with your future self.

Leave room for surprises by adding a little buffer to your estimates, and review your day briefly when you finish: what to keep, what to stop, what to start tomorrow. Batch similar tasks together to save your brain from constant switching. When procrastination shows up, shrink the first step until it feels too small to resist. Time management is not about scheduling every minute; it is about building light structure so your effort lands where it counts.

Chapter 16 — Set Goals & Plans

Goals turn wishes into action. Write one clear sentence that names what you want to achieve and how you will know it is done, then choose a date that gives you enough challenge to feel proud. Break the goal into weekly steps that you can actually do, and add small plan- B options for obstacles you can predict. Tie the goal to a value—why it matters to you—so your motivation has roots when the work gets dull.

Track progress on a simple chart and celebrate milestones with rewards that support the goal rather than distract from it. Show your plan to someone who can cheer you on and keep you honest when you want to give up. If a plan proves too heavy, adjust the steps, not the dream. Goals that are visible, measured, and connected to your values become maps you can follow, even when the trail bends.

Chapter 17 — Note- Taking

Good notes are a gift to your future self. Date and title each page so you can find ideas later, and listen for teacher signals like "the three causes" or "the main steps" to guide what you capture. Use short phrases and key words instead of full sentences so your hand can keep up with your brain. Leave a margin for questions, diagrams, and cues to help your memory lock onto what matters.

At the end of a lesson, write a quick summary in your own words, then review messy parts within a day while the ideas are still warm. Develop a simple symbol key for main ideas, results, and questions, and keep it on the inside cover of your notebook. Notes are not a transcript of every word you heard; they are a map to the learning. With steady habits, your notes become a study partner that never forgets.

Chapter 18 — Read for Meaning

Reading for meaning means you don't just move your eyes across words; you understand, connect, and remember. Before you dive in, preview the text by scanning the title, headings, visuals, and any guiding questions. Set a purpose—perhaps to find the main idea or to compare two viewpoints—so your attention knows what to hunt. Read in chunks, pausing to paraphrase what you just learned, and mark key terms or examples that answer your purpose.

Ask "why" and "how," not just "what." Connect new facts to something you already know so they have a hook to hang on. When a word is unfamiliar, use context to guess the meaning, then confirm it with a quick lookup. After you finish, summarize the text in a few sentences and explain it to someone else; teaching locks learning in place.

Chapter 19 — Memory Tricks

Memory improves with attention, organization, and smart repetition. Start by focusing well while you learn; what never enters the mind cannot be recalled later. Organize information into small, meaningful chunks—groups of facts that fit together—and link them to vivid images or stories so your brain has more paths to find them. Use acronyms, rhythms, or locations in a mental "memory palace" to store items in order.

Spacing your practice beats cramming because the brain strengthens memories each time it must reach for them. Review shortly after learning, then again after a day, then after a few days; each review can be brief because you are refreshing, not relearning. Teach someone else the idea in your own words, write it from memory, then check what you missed. Sleep, movement, and hydration help memory more than another hour of tired staring. Treat your brain like a friendly library: keep shelves tidy, visit often, and the book you need will be easier to find.

Chapter 20 — Test Prep & Test Day

Good preparation begins long before the test date. Clarify what will be covered and how questions will be asked, then build a small plan that spreads study across days. Use class notes, homework, and practice problems to target what matters most. Study in short, focused sessions, testing yourself rather than only rereading. When you miss something, mark it and return later so hard spots get extra attention. Prepare the practical things too—pencils, calculator, watch, water—so test day is not a scavenger hunt.

On the day itself, arrive a little early, breathe steadily, and preview the test to plan your time. Begin with questions you can do to build momentum, mark puzzles to revisit, and keep an eye on the clock without staring at it. If anxiety rises, pause for a few slow breaths and reset your attention to the task in front of you. When you finish, use extra minutes to check for small errors and to answer every question you can. Afterward, review what worked in your prep and what to change next time. Tests measure moments, not your worth; strong habits will outlast any single score.

Chapter 21 — Ask for Help

Asking for help is a smart way to move faster, not a sign that you are weak. Start by noticing the moment you feel stuck and naming it clearly: you can't find the next step, a concept won't click, or your plan is too big. Choose someone suited to the question—a teacher, coach, librarian, classmate, or family member—and arrive with context. Share what you've tried, where it broke down, and what kind of help you're hoping for so the other person can aim their support.

Be ready to listen, take notes, and try the suggestion right away, even if it feels small. Thank the person, report back on what worked, and keep building your "help network" for future projects. Sometimes help means learning where to look—an index, a database, a tutorial—so you can help yourself next time. If you hear "not now" or "I don't know," accept it with grace and ask who else might be a good guide. Courage plus curiosity is a powerful combo.

Chapter 22 — Project Planning

Good projects begin with a clear picture of the finished thing and a map that gets you there. Define the outcome in one sentence and work backward to today, marking the few steps that truly matter. Break heavy tasks into small, visible actions you can actually do in a short session. Put dates on milestones that make sense for your calendar, and plan simple check-ins to catch problems before they grow teeth.

Gather the resources you need, from tools and sources to people who can give feedback, then start early enough that surprises don't sink your work. Keep your plan flexible by adding a little buffer and a plan B for predictable obstacles. As you make progress, adjust the route rather than abandoning the goal, and capture what you learn so the next project starts stronger. A good plan doesn't cage creativity; it gives it a runway.

Chapter 23 — Digital Organization

A tidy digital life saves hours. Create a simple folder structure by class or activity, then name files so they sort themselves—date first, then topic and version, using clear words you can search later. Keep your desktop clear; it's a workspace, not a storage closet. Use cloud sync or a backup drive so a device problem doesn't erase hard work. When a file is final, archive it; when it's a draft, keep the version number honest.

Treat email and messages like a mailbox, not a to-do list. Read, reply if needed, and file or delete; star only the few items that truly require action. Put deadlines on a calendar you actually see. Once a week, spend a short session cleaning up downloads, renaming messy files, and tossing duplicates. Organization isn't about perfection—it's about being able to find what you need, when you need it, without stress.

Chapter 24 — Build a Reading Habit

Reading grows when it has a home in your day. Pick a daily time—after breakfast, on the bus, before bed—and protect it the way you protect a practice or rehearsal. Choose books at the right challenge level: not so easy you coast, not so hard you drown. Keep a small stack of "next reads" ready so finishing one book slides naturally into starting another, and let yourself stop a book that truly isn't working.

Mix purpose and pleasure. Read to learn something you care about and to relax into stories that lift your imagination. Visit the library, ask friends for recommendations, and talk about what you read so the habit has community. Track titles in a simple list or journal and notice patterns: which topics light you up, which authors make you think. A few pages every day beat a sprint once a month; consistency turns reading from task to treasure.

Home & Daily Life

Chapter 25 — Morning & Night Routines

Routines are the bookends that keep the rest of your day upright. Evenings are for setting tomorrow up to be kind: pack your bag, lay out clothes, charge devices, and look at the first appointment so the morning isn't a scramble. Add a short wind-down—stretching, light reading, or gentle music—to tell your body, "We're closing for the night." The more decisions you remove before bedtime, the easier the next day begins.

Mornings work best when they start the same way most days. Wake at a steady time, get a sip of water and some light, move your body a little, and do the first important task before distractions wake up. Routines are not rigid schedules; they are rails that keep you from sliding off track. Adjust them when seasons change, and return to them when life gets messy. Small, steady steps create calm momentum.

Chapter 26 — Tidy Your Room

A tidy room is a tool: it saves time, lowers stress, and gives your brain clear space to think. Create simple "homes" for the things you use most—books here, supplies there, a bin for odds and ends—and practice returning items to their home when you finish. Keep a hamper for laundry, a small trash can, and a donation box for the things you've outgrown so clutter has fewer places to hide.

Make your bed each morning to flip the room from "sleep" to "ready." Do a two-minute reset most evenings: clear surfaces, put shoes where they live, and empty the backpack of scraps and crumbs. Once a week, do a slightly deeper pass—dust, vacuum, and check under the bed for runaway socks and mystery items. Tidy is not about fancy bins; it's about simple habits that make your space work for you.

Chapter 27 — Laundry Basics

Laundry is easier when you respect the steps. Sort by color and fabric—lights with lights, darks with darks, towels with towels—and check labels for special care. Treat stains promptly by blotting, not rubbing, and read detergent instructions so you don't waste soap or damage clothes. Choose water temperature to match the load, and avoid overfilling the machine so water and soap can actually do their job.

When the cycle ends, shake items out, hang or lay delicate pieces to dry if needed, and move the rest to the dryer with a clean lint filter. Folding is faster than hunting through a basket each morning; pair socks, stack shirts, and store outfits where you can grab them. Return clean clothes to their homes the same day so piles don't become furniture. A little care now saves "nothing to wear" later.

Chapter 28 — Simple Sewing Fixes

Basic sewing lets you rescue clothes instead of replacing them. Learn to thread a needle, knot the end, and make small, even stitches that hold without puckering fabric. Practice on scrap cloth first, then try reattaching a button, closing a tiny seam opening, or making a quick hem so pants stop dragging. Keep a small kit with needles, thread in neutral colors, scissors, safety pins, and a few spare buttons.

Work slowly with good light, and keep fingers clear of sharp points. If you're young, ask an adult to supervise until you're steady with the tools, and store everything safely when you finish. Not every repair needs to be invisible; it just needs to be secure and comfortable. These small skills teach patience and save money, and they make your clothes feel like something you can care for, not just consume.

Chapter 29 — Kitchen Safety

The kitchen is fun and full of hazards, so safety comes first. Tie back long hair, roll sleeves, and wash hands before you touch food. Use a cutting board and keep the blade moving away from fingers. Keep raw meat and ready-to-eat foods apart, and clean knives and surfaces that touched raw ingredients before you touch anything else. Turn pot handles inward, step back from popping oil, and use dry oven mitts around heat.

Always cook with adult supervision until you've been trained for the tasks you're doing. Read a recipe all the way through before starting so you're not surprised by a step that needs time or special equipment. Wipe spills right away to prevent slips, keep cords and towels away from burners, and never leave heat unattended. Safety is the best ingredient; it keeps meals delicious and memories happy.

Chapter 30 — Make a Simple Breakfast

Breakfast fuels your morning, and simple doesn't mean boring. A balanced plate might include whole grains, a source of protein, and fruit or vegetables. You could build yogurt with fruit and a sprinkle of oats, scramble eggs to serve with toast and tomatoes, or simmer oatmeal and stir in nuts and cinnamon. Start by washing hands, gathering ingredients, and setting out the tools so you're not racing around the kitchen.

Move at a calm pace and taste as you go so you learn what you like. Clean as you work by putting peels and wrappers into a bin, rinsing tools between tasks, and wiping the counter before you sit down to eat. Afterward, wash dishes and return everything to its home so the kitchen is ready for the next cook—maybe you, at lunchtime. A simple, steady breakfast routine is a kindness to your future self.

Chapter 31 — Read a Recipe & Measure

Recipes are stories with actions, so read the whole story first. Notice the ingredient list, the order of steps, and any times and temperatures that require patience. Set up your space with ingredients measured and ready, a habit known as "mise en place," so cooking feels smooth rather than chaotic. Preheat the oven or pan on time, and start steps that take longer earlier in the process so everything finishes together.

Measure carefully. Use liquid measuring cups for liquids and flat spoons or dry cups for dry ingredients, and level the top so amounts are accurate. Some recipes welcome substitutions; others, especially baked goods, rely on precision. When in doubt, follow the instructions the first time, then experiment once you understand the basics. Careful reading and measuring turn you from a follower of recipes into a confident cook.

Chapter 32 — Food Safety & Storage

Good food safety keeps meals joyful. Begin with clean hands, clean tools, and clean surfaces. Keep raw and ready- to- eat foods separate from start to finish, and use fresh plates for cooked items so juices don't travel the wrong direction. Chill leftovers promptly in clean containers, label them with the date, and store them where cool air can move around them. Reheat thoroughly and avoid guessing with foods that seem "iffy."

Pay attention to smell, texture, and appearance, and follow local guidelines for how long different foods can be safely stored. When unsure, throw it out; saving a few bites is never worth a stomachache. Ask an adult to teach you the household rules for storage and reheating, and use them every time. Food safety is mostly about steady habits—simple steps that become automatic and keep everyone well.

Chapter 33 — Wash Dishes & Clean Up

Cleaning up is part of cooking, and doing it well keeps the kitchen a place people love to use. Start by scraping leftovers into the compost or trash and giving pans a quick soak so stuck bits loosen. Wash from cleanest to dirtiest so water stays useful longer: glasses and utensils first, then plates and bowls, with greasy pans last. Rinse and set items to dry on a rack or towel, or load the dishwasher according to the machine's layout.

Wipe counters, stove tops, and table spaces, sweeping crumbs down and out rather than around and around. Squeeze out sponges, hang towels to dry, and empty the trash if it's full so smells don't linger. Return tools to their homes so the next cook starts fresh. Clean-as-you-go makes the end of the meal light work, and it teaches respect for shared spaces and the people who use them.

Chapter 34 — Bathroom Cleaning

Bathrooms feel better when they're clean and fresh. Start by opening a window or using a fan for airflow, then put on gloves if you're using cleaners. Clear counters, dust from high to low, and work in an order that keeps dirty water from revisiting clean places. Scrub the sink, faucet, and handles; wipe mirrors with a streak- free cloth; tackle the toilet with dedicated tools; and finish with the tub or shower so soap and hair don't wander back.

Use cleaners exactly as directed and never mix products, especially those containing bleach and ammonia. Rinse and dry surfaces so soap residue doesn't invite grime back early. Replace towels, restock paper and soap, and mop or vacuum the floor last so you leave the room truly finished. A weekly routine keeps the job small; a monthly deeper clean prevents surprises. Clean bathrooms are a quiet kindness to everyone in the house.

Chapter 35 — Care for Your Stuff

Taking care of your things extends their life and saves money. Label items that travel—water bottles, notebooks, jackets—so lost goods can find their way home. Keep electronics off the floor, wrap cords gently, and store devices where heat and spills can't reach them. For shoes, backpacks, and sports gear, let them dry fully between uses and clean them according to the material so they don't break down early.

Do small maintenance before small problems grow teeth: tighten a loose screw, tape a fraying cable properly, and check zippers before they stick. Keep manuals or quick photos of model numbers for future repairs, and learn when to ask for help from a grown- up or a repair shop. Share respectfully when you borrow and return items on time. Caring for your stuff is really caring for your time and attention.

Chapter 36 — Host a Guest Nicely

Hosting is the art of making someone feel welcome. Tidy the space they'll see first, set out a place to sit, and plan a simple activity or conversation starter so nobody has to wonder what to do. Greet your guest at the door with a smile, offer water or a snack if that's the household custom, and explain any house rules in a friendly way—shoes off here, pets are shy, bathroom down the hall.

During the visit, include your guest in choices and check that they're comfortable. Keep phones away unless you're using them together for a purpose, and end on time so people leave feeling good. Afterward, help clean up and send a short thank-you message if they hosted next time. Good hosting isn't fancy; it's attention, warmth, and a plan that fits your space and your guest.

Health & Body

Chapter 37 — Handwashing & Germs

Clean hands are one of the simplest ways to stay healthy. Wash with soap and water before eating or cooking, after using the bathroom, after touching animals or outdoor surfaces, and whenever hands look or feel dirty. Rub all parts—palms, backs, between fingers, fingertips, and thumbs—for enough time to do a short song, then rinse and dry with a clean towel. When sinks are out of reach, use sanitizer as a backup and wash properly when you can.

Cover coughs and sneezes into your elbow, avoid touching your face with unwashed hands, and stay home when you're sick so others can stay well. Keep shared items and surfaces reasonably clean, especially during cold and flu seasons. Local health guidance should always lead the way; when in doubt, ask a trusted adult. Small, steady habits protect you and your community.

Chapter 38 — Teeth Care

Your smile is part of your health. Brush gently twice a day with a fluoride toothpaste, covering every surface of every tooth and the gumline, and take your time so the work is complete. Floss once a day to clean where brushes can't reach, and swish with water after snacks when a full brushing isn't possible. Drink plenty of water, especially after eating, and save very sugary foods and drinks for less frequent moments.

Protect teeth during sports with a properly fitted mouthguard, and visit a dental professional on the schedule they recommend for cleanings and checkups. If something hurts or feels loose, say so early; small issues are easier to fix than big ones. Your habits matter more than fancy tools. For personalized advice, follow your dentist's guidance and the recommendations where you live.

Chapter 39 — Protect Your Skin

Skin protects everything beneath it, so treat it kindly. Seek shade during the strongest sun, wear hats and clothing that cover well, and use a broad- spectrum sunscreen as directed on the label, reapplying as needed. In cold or windy weather, cover exposed skin and use a gentle moisturizer to prevent chapping. Rinse off sweat and dirt after play so pores can breathe, and change out of wet clothes quickly to stay comfortable.

Use bug protection when needed and learn which local plants can irritate skin so you can avoid them. Try new products on a small patch first in case your skin is sensitive, and ask a trusted adult or healthcare professional if you notice rashes, burns, or anything that doesn't heal. Good habits plus local guidance keep your skin doing its job as your first line of defense.

Chapter 40 — Sleep Smart

Sleep is not lost time; it's when your brain files memories, your body repairs itself, and your mood resets. Aim for a steady schedule that lets you wake without an alarm most days, and build a gentle wind-down in the hour before bed: dim lights, quiet activities, and screens set aside. Keep your room cool, dark, and calm, and reserve the bed for sleep so your brain links that space with rest rather than homework or scrolling.

If worries whirl at night, write them on a notepad and promise your brain you'll handle them tomorrow. Get morning light and movement to anchor your internal clock, and keep naps short and early if you take them at all. When sleep is hard for many nights in a row, talk with a trusted adult and follow local health advice. Good sleep makes everything else easier—learning, friendships, sports, and joy.

Chapter 41 — Move Your Body

Your body was built to move, and movement helps everything else work better—mood, sleep, learning, and strength.

Aim to sprinkle activity through your day: walk fast enough to feel your heart wake up, climb stairs, dance while you tidy, kick a ball, ride a bike, or practice a sport you enjoy. Variety keeps you interested and trains different muscles, so mix balance, flexibility, and strength with play. Warm up gently before tougher efforts, listen to your body's signals, and progress in small steps so today's challenge becomes tomorrow's normal.

Consistency matters more than intensity. A little movement most days beats a hard burst once a month. Set small goals you can actually keep, like stretching after homework or shooting ten baskets before dinner. Fuel with water, wear shoes that support you, and rest when you need to—recovery is part of training. When moving with others, share space safely and cheer effort, not just wins. The more you move, the more energy you'll have to keep moving.

Chapter 42 — Balanced Plate

Food is fuel and also culture, comfort, and celebration. A balanced plate usually includes a colorful mix of vegetables and fruits, a source of protein like beans, eggs, yogurt, tofu, fish, or lean meats, and grains such as rice, pasta, or bread—whole grains when you can. Healthy fats from foods like nuts, seeds, or olive oil help your body use vitamins and keep you satisfied. Portion sizes change with age, activity, and local guidance, so learn what works for you and follow the recommendations where you live.

Eat slowly enough to notice flavors and fullness, and drink water with meals so your body can do its work. Try new foods alongside familiar favorites, and keep enjoying the dishes that matter in your family's traditions. Planning simple snacks—fruit, yogurt, vegetables with a dip—keeps you from arriving at meals too hungry. Balanced eating is not about perfection; it's about steady choices that help you feel strong and ready for your day.

Chapter 43 — Drink Enough Water

Water carries nutrients, cools you down, cushions joints, and helps your brain think clearly. Keep a reusable bottle nearby and sip across the day, adding more when you're active, it's hot, or you're wearing lots of gear. Notice how your body feels when you're well hydrated—steady energy, fewer headaches, easier focus—and use that feeling as a guide. As a rough check, pale straw-colored urine often means you're getting enough, while darker colors can signal it's time to drink more.

Choose water first and save sugary drinks for occasional moments if your family uses them. Foods like fruit and soups also add to hydration, but plain water is simple and dependable. If you forget to drink, link sips to habits you already have: after brushing teeth, at class breaks, or when you put on your shoes. Follow local health advice for specific needs and ask a trusted adult if you're unsure. Small sips, repeated often, keep your whole system running smoothly.

Chapter 44 — Name Your Feelings

Emotions are signals, not problems to hide. When you name a feeling—"I feel worried about the test," "I feel excited for the game"—you turn noise into information your brain can use. Notice where feelings live in your body: a tight chest, a light bounce, a heavy stomach. Try putting them into a short sentence that links feeling to cause: "I feel frustrated because the project is confusing." Naming feelings clearly helps you choose better next steps and helps others know how to support you.

Feelings change like weather; they pass more easily when you acknowledge them and treat them with respect. If you struggle to find the right word, think in families of emotions—sadness, anger, fear, joy, surprise, shame—and then choose the closer match. Share feelings with people you trust and listen to theirs in return. Emotional words are tools; the more you can reach for the right one, the more skillfully you can build your day.

Chapter 45 — Calm-Down Skills

Everyone needs ways to settle a stirred-up mind and body. Slow breathing is a powerful start: lengthen your exhales, count gently, and let your shoulders drop as if they're melting. Ground your attention by naming things you can see, hear, and feel in the room, or by pressing your feet into the floor and noticing the support beneath you. Movement helps too—walk a quiet lap, stretch your hands and back, or shake out tension from fingers to shoulders.

Thoughts matter as much as breath. Speak to yourself the way a kind coach would: "This is tough, and I can handle tough things." If you need space, take a short break and return when your thinking is clearer. Music, drawing, or journaling can give feelings somewhere safe to go. Practice calming skills when you're already okay so they're ready in moments you really need them. You're training your nervous system to choose steady over stormy.

Chapter 46 — When Sad or Angry

Sadness and anger visit everyone. They often show up when something important feels lost or unfair, and they deserve honest attention. Start by noticing and naming the feeling without judging yourself for having it. Give the emotion a safe path: talk with someone you trust, write it down, cry if you need to, or put the energy into healthy movement like a walk or a run. Anger especially wants action—choose actions that don't harm people or things, and step back from situations until you can respond, not react.

If heavy feelings linger or keep returning, ask for help from a caring adult or a health professional who can guide you, and follow local advice for getting support. Sleep, meals, sunshine, and connection make a real difference. Avoid choices that try to numb feelings in ways that cause new problems. You are not your emotion; you are the person noticing it and choosing your next step. With practice and support, waves of feeling pass, and you grow stronger at surfing them.

Chapter 47 — Personal Hygiene

Clean habits protect health and help you feel confident. Bathe or shower regularly, especially after sports or hot weather, and wash areas where sweat collects. Brush teeth twice a day and floss daily, trim nails, and wash hair as often as your scalp and activities require. Change into clean clothes, socks, and underwear, and let shoes and gear dry out between uses so odors and bacteria don't take hold. Keep a small kit in your bag with tissues, sanitizer, a comb, and other items you find helpful.

As bodies grow and change, you may notice new needs like deodorant or skincare routines; ask a trusted adult for guidance that fits your age and your local recommendations. During monthly cycles, learn the products and schedules that work for your body and dispose of items properly. Hygiene is less about looking perfect and more about caring for yourself and for people who share your space. A few steady habits keep you fresh, comfortable, and ready.

Chapter 48 — Body Safety Basics

Your body belongs to you, and you have the right to feel safe in it. Learn to trust your early signals of discomfort and speak clearly: "Please stop," "I don't like that," or "No." Ask before touching others and expect the same respect in return. Private areas, often described as parts covered by a swimsuit, are private for everyone; if someone asks to see or touch your private parts, or asks you to keep a touch a secret, tell a trusted adult right away, even if the person is someone you know. Safe adults will help you and won't blame you.

Make a short list of trusted adults and places you can go if you feel unsafe—family members, teachers, coaches, or neighbors—and practice how you would ask for help. If someone ignores your “no,” move to safety as soon as you can and keep telling until you receive support. Body safety is not about fear; it’s about clear rules that protect dignity. You deserve safety, respect, and care.

Safety & First Aid

Chapter 49 — Your Address and Emergency Numbers

In an emergency, clear information saves time. Memorize your full name, home address, nearby landmarks, and the phone numbers for your parents or guardians. Learn which emergency number your country uses—such as 911, 112, or another—and how to reach it from your phone. Practice saying, calmly and slowly, what happened, where you are, and whether anyone is hurt, then follow the dispatcher's instructions and stay on the line unless you're told to hang up.

Only call emergency services for real emergencies like a fire, someone who is seriously hurt, or a dangerous situation. Prank calls can delay help for people who truly need it and may have serious consequences. Keep addresses and key numbers posted in a visible place at home and saved in your contacts.

Chapter 50 — Fire Safety and Escape

Fire moves fast, so planning ahead matters. Make sure smoke alarms in your home are tested on the schedule recommended where you live, and learn how they sound. With your family, plan two ways out of each sleeping area if possible, choose an outdoor meeting spot, and practice getting there so everyone knows the route. Keep hallways clear, sleep with doors closed if that's the local safety advice, and know how to unlock windows that are meant to open.

If you see smoke indoors, stay low where the air is clearer, feel doors with the back of your hand before opening them, and use a different way out if a door is hot. If clothing catches fire, stop, drop, and roll until the flames are out, then cool the skin with water and get help. Never go back inside a burning building for any reason; share information with firefighters instead.

Chapter 51 — Water Safety

Water is fun and powerful, and safety keeps it joyful. Learn to swim with a qualified instructor if you can, and always swim with an adult watching closely. Wear a properly fitted life jacket when boating or near deep, moving, or uncertain water, and follow posted rules at pools, lakes, and beaches. Enter unfamiliar water feet first, watch for sudden drop-offs, and be cautious of currents and waves that can tire even strong swimmers.

At home, keep younger children within arm's reach in bathtubs and small pools, and empty buckets and kiddie pools after use so they don't become hazards. Walk, don't run, on wet surfaces to avoid falls, and keep long hair tied back near drains or jets. If someone is in trouble, call for help and reach or throw something that floats rather than jumping in unless you are trained for rescues. Respect for water's power is the foundation of safe fun.

Chapter 52 — Weather Safety

Weather can change quickly, so paying attention helps you stay ready. Learn your area's common weather risks and the alerts used by local authorities, then follow their guidance when warnings appear. During thunderstorms, go indoors when you hear thunder and avoid tall isolated trees, open fields, and water. In extreme heat, rest in shade or cool places, drink water, and watch for signs of overheating. In cold weather, dress in layers that stay dry and cover fingers, toes, and ears; change out of wet clothes quickly.

Make simple plans at home for outages or storms—flashlights with fresh batteries, a small supply of water and shelf-stable food, and a safe place to wait out severe conditions if your region needs one. Keep devices charged when big storms are forecast and check on neighbors who may need help.

Chapter 53 — Street and Bike Safety

Streets demand attention and respect. Cross at corners or crosswalks when you can, make eye contact with drivers, and look left, right, and left again before stepping off the curb. Put phones away and remove headphones so you can hear and react. Wear bright or reflective clothing in low light, and be ready to stop if a moving car, bike, or scooter surprises you.

On a bike, wear a properly fitted helmet every ride and choose a route that matches your skill. Ride predictably, follow local traffic rules, and be visible with lights or reflectors when required. Keep your bike in good repair—working brakes and properly inflated tires make every ride safer. When walking, riding, or scooting with friends, take care of one another by calling out obstacles and waiting at crossings.

Chapter 54 — Public Transport Basics

Buses, trains, and trams move lots of people efficiently when everyone follows simple courtesies. Wait behind safety lines, stand back from curbs and platform edges, and let passengers exit before you enter. Have your fare, pass, or ticket ready so boarding is smooth, and move down the aisle to make space for others. If you're standing, hold a rail and plant your feet to handle starts and stops.

Stay aware of your surroundings and keep bags zipped and close to your body. Offer seats to people who may need them more—older adults, pregnant people, or those with disabilities—and use a quiet voice on calls. Know your stop ahead of time and signal or move toward the door so you can exit safely. If you ever feel unsafe, move near the driver or a group, and tell a staff member.

Chapter 55 — Internet Safety and Privacy

The internet connects you to ideas and people, and it also carries risks. Protect your accounts with strong, unique passwords and privacy settings that match your family's rules. Be careful with personal information; avoid sharing your full name, address, school, phone number, or real-time location with people you don't know offline. Think before you post, because words and images can travel far and last a long time.

Treat others online with the same kindness and boundaries you use in person. If you see bullying, report it and save evidence; if someone makes you uncomfortable, block and tell a trusted adult. Watch for scams that pretend to be friends, prizes, or official messages asking for money or codes. Balance screen time with sleep, movement, and real- world relationships.

Chapter 56 — First Aid: Cuts and Scrapes

Small cuts and scrapes are part of active life. Begin by cleaning your hands, then rinse the wound gently under clean running water to remove dirt. If needed, wash around the area with mild soap, taking care not to drive soap into the wound. Apply gentle pressure with a clean cloth or bandage to stop bleeding, then cover the area with a sterile bandage or dressing that keeps out dirt while it heals. Change the covering if it gets wet or dirty and keep an eye on how the skin looks.

If the wound is deep, won't stop bleeding after you apply pressure, was caused by something dirty or rusty, or shows signs of infection such as warmth, swelling, red streaks, or pus, tell an adult and follow local medical advice right away. Avoid picking scabs so your body can repair itself. Store basic supplies in a simple kit and learn where they live at home or school. Calm, clean care helps your skin do the rest.

Chapter 57 — First Aid: Nosebleeds and Splinters

For a nosebleed, stay calm, sit up, and lean slightly forward so blood doesn't go down your throat. Pinch the soft part of your nose just below the bridge and breathe through your mouth, holding steady pressure for the amount of time recommended by local guidance; peeking too early can restart bleeding. Avoid tilting your head back. After the bleeding stops, rest and try not to blow your nose or bend over for a while. If bleeding is heavy, keeps coming back, or follows an injury, tell an adult and seek professional advice.

For a small splinter, wash your hands and the area, clean tweezers with alcohol if available, and gently pull the splinter out in the same direction it went in. Rinse again and cover with a small bandage if needed. If the splinter is deep, near the eye, or hard to remove, don't dig—ask an adult for help. Watch for redness or pain that grows, and follow local health guidance. Simple tools and patience keep small problems small.

Chapter 58 — When to Call for Help

Calling for help is a brave and smart action when a situation is bigger than you. Seek an adult immediately and contact emergency services if someone is unconscious, struggling to breathe, bleeding heavily, showing signs of a serious allergic reaction, has a possible broken bone or head injury, if there is a fire or smoke, or if you feel unsafe because of a crime or dangerous situation. If you must call yourself, speak clearly: your name, location, what happened, and how many people need help. Follow the dispatcher's instructions and stay on the line.

Not every problem is an emergency, but many still need help. If you're worried about someone's health or safety, or your own, tell a trusted adult even if you're not sure how serious it is. It's better to ask than to guess. Keep important numbers handy at home and on your phone, and learn the fastest way to reach local help where you live. Quick, calm action can make a big difference.

Chapter 59 — Household Hazards

Homes feel safe, yet they contain items that need care. Keep medicines, cleaning products, batteries, and small objects that could be swallowed stored high, locked, or out of reach according to local safety advice. Treat tools, matches, lighters, and sharp objects with respect and only use them with training and adult supervision. Hot surfaces and liquids can burn, cords can trip, and heavy furniture can tip if climbed—slow down, look around, and move thoughtfully.

Learn to read safety labels and follow instructions on products and appliances. Unplug devices by the plug, not the cord, and keep drinks away from electronics. Clean up spills to prevent slips, and keep floors clear so exits are easy to reach. If something smells strange or a device acts oddly, tell an adult and step back. Safety at home is mostly about awareness, storage, and steady habits that prevent surprises.

Chapter 60 — Poisonous Plants

Plants are beautiful, and some can irritate skin or make you sick if touched or eaten. The safest rule is simple: do not eat plants, berries, or mushrooms you find outdoors unless a knowledgeable adult tells you they are safe. Learn the poisonous plants that grow in your area from reliable local sources, and give them space when you see them. After hiking or yard work, wash hands and skin, and change clothes if you think you brushed against a plant that causes a rash.

Teach younger children and visitors the same caution, and keep pets away from plants that can harm them. If sap or hairs from a plant get on your skin, rinse with plenty of water as soon as you can and tell an adult; if you have a strong reaction or if someone swallows a plant, follow local emergency or poison control guidance right away. Knowing what grows around you—and respecting it—keeps outdoor adventures safe and enjoyable.

Nature & Outdoors

Chapter 61 — Dress for the Weather

Clothing is gear, and the right gear keeps you comfortable and safe. Start by checking the forecast and thinking in layers. A light, sweat-moving layer next to your skin keeps you dry; a warm middle layer holds heat; and an outer layer blocks wind and rain. In strong sun, wear a brimmed hat, sunglasses if you use them, and clothing that covers well. In cold or windy weather, protect fingers, toes, and ears, and change out of wet clothes quickly so you don't lose heat. Good shoes that match the day—waterproof for puddles, sturdy for trails, breathable for heat—make every step better.

Bring small extras when the day might change: an extra layer, a compact rain shell, or dry socks in a zip bag. Materials matter more than fashion; wool or synthetics manage moisture better than heavy cotton when you're active. Pack sunscreen and lip balm if your family uses them, drink water, and listen to your body's signals. Dressing for the weather is not about being tough;

it's about being prepared so you can enjoy whatever the day brings.

Chapter 62 — Read a Simple Map

Maps are models of places that let you plan and explore without getting lost. Begin by finding the map's compass rose so you know which way is north, then match the map to the real world by turning it until features line up with what you see. Read the legend to learn what symbols mean—trails, water, parks, buildings—and notice the scale so you can estimate distances. Landmarks like a river bend, a bridge, or a tall building become anchors you can spot in both the map and the landscape.

Before a trip, trace your route with a finger, counting turns and noting big features along the way. While moving, check the map at calm moments so small mistakes stay small, and update your plan if you meet a closed path or a detour. Phone maps are helpful, yet it's wise to learn paper too in case batteries fade or signals vanish. A good map reader doesn't guess.

Chapter 63 — Hike Smart

A smart hike begins long before your first step. Choose a trail that matches your group's experience, check the forecast, and tell a trusted adult where you're going and when you expect to return. Wear comfortable shoes, pack water and snacks, and bring a small kit with basics like a bandage, a whistle, and a light if your family uses them. Start at a steady pace so you can finish strong, and stay on marked paths to protect nature and your safety.

As you walk, notice trail signs, share space kindly, and give wildlife plenty of room. Step carefully on wet rocks and loose gravel, and turn back if weather or daylight changes the plan. If you realize you're lost, stop, breathe, and think; look and listen for familiar features, and use your map or phone as available. Signal with your voice or whistle if you need help. A good hike is measured in smiles and scenery, not just miles.

Chapter 64 — Leave No Trace

The outdoors belongs to everyone, including future visitors and the plants and animals who live there now. "Leave No Trace" means enjoying nature while protecting it. Plan ahead so you bring what you need, stay on durable surfaces to avoid damaging fragile areas, and carry out all your trash—including peels and crumbs—so animals don't learn to depend on human food. Leave rocks, flowers, and artifacts where you find them so others can discover them too.

Keep a respectful distance from wildlife and watch quietly instead of chasing for a better view. If fires are allowed where you live and hike, follow local rules or skip fires entirely; many places are safer without them. Be considerate of other visitors by keeping voices low, sharing narrow trails, and giving room to people who are passing. When you leave a place, it should look the same or better than when you arrived. That's how we say thank you to nature.

Chapter 65 — Notice Animal Signs

Animals often tell their stories without showing their faces. Look for tracks in mud or snow and notice the shape, size, and pattern of steps to guess who passed by. Listen for calls and rustles at dawn or dusk, and watch for nests, burrows, feathers, and chewed leaves that hint at recent visitors. Scat—animal droppings—can reveal diet and species if you observe from a respectful distance. A small notebook or photo helps you compare what you see with a guide later.

Move slowly, keep voices soft, and give animals space so they can keep living their lives without stress. Never chase, feed, or corner wildlife; human food can harm them, and close contact can be risky for both sides. The more time you spend noticing signs, the better your eyes and ears become at reading a landscape. You won't just see an empty field; you'll see a busy neighborhood with quiet, furry neighbors.

Chapter 66 — Plant a Seed

Planting a seed is patient magic. Choose a container with drainage or a sunny spot in the ground, fill it with good soil, and place the seed at the depth the packet suggests. Water gently so the soil is moist but not soggy, then keep the spot warm and bright according to the plant's needs. Germination can take days or weeks; checking daily and recording changes turns waiting into learning. Label what you planted so you remember which is which.

As the seedling grows, give it light, water, and time, turning the pot so stems grow straight and strong. When roots fill the pot, transplant carefully to a larger home and tuck the soil around it like a blanket. Watch for pests and problems, and learn the difference between overwatering and thirst. Harvest herbs, flowers, or vegetables with thanks, and add scraps to a compost if your household uses one. Growing a plant teaches care, cycles, and the quiet joy of tending life.

Chapter 67 — Pet Care Basics

Pets are family members, not toys, and they depend on you for daily care. Before bringing one home, learn what the species needs for space, food, exercise, and companionship, and make sure your whole household agrees to the plan. Fresh water, appropriate food, and a clean living area come first, followed by play, training, and gentle handling so the pet feels safe. Regular grooming and attention to nails, teeth, and coats help prevent problems.

Schedule checkups with a veterinarian as your family and local guidance recommend, and watch for changes in appetite, energy, or behavior that might signal a health issue. Keep identification tags or other approved ID on pets that go outdoors, and make a plan for who cares for the pet during trips. Trcat animals with patience and respect, and learn to read their signals so you know when they want attention and when they need space. A well- cared- for pet gives love and teaches responsibility every day.

Chapter 68 — Clouds and Forecast

The sky is a giant weather map. Puffy cumulus clouds often signal fair weather, high wispy cirrus can mean a change is coming, flat gray stratus may bring a light, steady rain, and tall, dark cumulonimbus can mean thunderstorms. Watch how clouds grow and move, feel the wind, and notice how the air smells before weather shifts. These clues won't replace official forecasts, but they deepen your understanding of what the day might do.

Check local forecasts from reliable sources to plan clothing and activities, and follow safety advice for your area. During stormy seasons, keep an eye on alerts and be ready to move inside if thunder, lightning, or severe winds approach. Track patterns in a simple weather journal—temperature, cloud type, wind, and what actually happened—to sharpen your prediction skills. The more attention you pay to the sky, the more it will teach you.

Chapter 69 — Know Your Neighborhood

Knowing where you live builds confidence and safety. Learn the names of nearby streets, parks, and landmarks, and practice safe routes to school, the library, and trusted friends' homes. Notice where crosswalks, bus stops, and public buildings are, and identify places you can go for help if you ever need it. A simple hand-drawn map of your daily world helps you remember details and share them with others.

Say hello to neighbors when your family says it's appropriate and learn community rhythms—when people walk dogs, where kids play, and which areas are busy or quiet. Pay attention to posted signs and local rules that keep spaces clean and friendly. With adult guidance, participate in neighborhood events or cleanups to help your area thrive. Familiarity turns streets from unknown lines into a place you belong.

Chapter 70 — Pack a Day Bag

A well-packed day bag makes small adventures easy. Start with water and a simple snack, then add an extra layer or a light rain shell if weather might change. Include sun protection your family uses, a small packable tote for unexpected items, and a basic first- aid item like a bandage if that's part of your household routine. Keep ID and emergency contact information where you can reach it quickly.

Choose a bag that fits comfortably on your shoulders and organize with small pockets so keys, transit cards, and a phone don't hide. If you're going farther, tell someone where you're headed and when you plan to return. Pack only what you'll use so the bag stays light enough to carry without strain. With a ready bag by the door, you can say "yes" to more of the day.

Money & Future

Chapter 71 — Save, Spend, Share

Money learns good habits just like people do. A simple way to start is to divide what you receive into three parts: some to **save** for future you, some to **spend** on needs and small wants, and some to **share** with causes or people you care about. Label jars or accounts so the plan is visible, then move money the moment you receive it. Watching the save jar grow teaches patience; choosing what to spend on teaches priorities; giving teaches gratitude and empathy.

Review your choices each month with a trusted adult. Did your saving move you toward a goal? Did your spending match what matters most? Did your sharing feel meaningful? Adjust the percentages as your needs change, and celebrate small wins like reaching a mini-goal or making someone's day through a kind gift. The save-spend-share habit builds balance that lasts long after the jars are empty and refilled.

Chapter 72 — Set a Savings Goal

Goals give your money a job. Picture something specific you want in the future—a book series, sports gear, a class, or part of a trip—and write the cost. Decide what you can save each week or month, and circle the date when you'll likely reach it. Post a simple chart and color a box every time you add money so progress feels real. If the goal is big, break it into steps with small celebrations along the way.

Protect your goal from impulse buys by using a pause rule: wait a day before spending on something not in your plan. Ask if there's a smarter way to reach the same joy—borrowing, buying used, or choosing a smaller version. Check in with a trusted adult about safe places to store savings. When you reach your target, enjoy the result and notice the skills you built: patience, planning, and pride.

Chapter 73 — Smart Shopping

Smart shoppers match money to values and needs. Before you buy, ask whether this is a need or a want, and whether there's a better use for the money. Compare options for quality and total cost, not just the price on the tag—how long will it last, what care does it need, and what are the return or warranty rules? Look for unit prices on shelf labels to compare sizes fairly, and consider trusted reviews rather than flashy ads.

Impulse fades when you slow down. Use a short waiting period for non-essentials and see if the desire remains. Think about second-hand or borrowing for items you'll use briefly, and take care of what you already own so you replace less. Keep receipts and check them for accuracy. Smart shopping is not about never buying; it's about buying with attention so your money does work you're proud of.

Chapter 74 — Price Tags and Receipts

Price tags tell part of the story. In many places, sales tax or other fees are added at checkout, so the amount you pay can be higher than the tag shows. Discounts, coupons, or promotions can also change the total, and unit price labels help you compare value across different sizes. Knowing these details helps you plan and avoid surprises at the register.

Receipts are your record of what happened. Check them for mistakes while you're still in the store and keep them in a safe place, especially for items you might return or that have warranties. Receipts also help you track spending in a notebook or budget app with a trusted adult. Understanding price tags and receipts turns shopping from guessing into informed choices.

Chapter 75 — Simple Budget

A budget is a plan for money you expect to receive and money you expect to spend. List your sources—allowance, small jobs, gifts—and then list regular costs like savings contributions, transportation, snacks, or activities. Set amounts that fit your reality and leave room for small surprises. At the end of the week or month, compare your plan to what actually happened and adjust the next plan so it's more accurate.

Think of a budget as a map you redraw as you learn new roads. If you overspend in one area, choose where to spend less next time or increase income if that's possible and allowed. If you underspend, decide whether to save the difference or move it to a higher- value use. The habit of planning, checking, and adjusting teaches control and reduces stress. The numbers are small now; the skills are huge.

Chapter 76 — Earn Your First Dollar

Earning money teaches effort, responsibility, and value. Look for age- appropriate tasks that help others—watering plants, pet sitting with an adult, tutoring a younger student, raking leaves, or helping at events—always following family rules and local laws. Start with a clear agreement about the job, time, and pay, then do the work carefully and on schedule. Be polite, communicate if plans change, and say thank you when you're paid.

Keep a simple record of earnings and any costs, like supplies, so you know what you actually made. Save a portion toward a goal, set aside a little for giving if that's your habit, and enjoy a thoughtful spend. The best way to get repeat work is to be reliable and kind. Your first dollar isn't just money—it's a story about trust and skill that you can keep building.

Chapter 77 — Banking Basics

Banks and credit unions offer safe places to keep money and tools to manage it. With a trusted adult, learn about savings accounts that may earn interest—a small reward for keeping money there—and how deposits and withdrawals work. Get to know basic terms like balance, statement, and transfer, and ask how to avoid fees. Keep your login details and PIN private, and use strong passwords to protect your account.

Many people also use digital tools to check balances, set savings goals, or move small amounts between jars or accounts.

Whether you use cash or cards, track what you spend so the number in your head matches the number in your account. Separate money meant for saving from money meant for spending to avoid mix-ups. Banking isn't magic; it's organized storage plus simple math, and you can learn it step by step.

Chapter 78 — Give and Volunteer

Giving is a way to share your time, talents, and resources with your community. Choose causes that matter to you—animals, libraries, parks, food support—and learn what they actually need. Sometimes the best gift is money; sometimes it's a few hours sorting donations, reading with younger kids, or cleaning a trail with a group. When you volunteer, arrive on time, listen to instructions, and finish tasks with care so your help truly helps.

Small, steady acts add up. Set aside a portion of your money for giving if that's part of your family's values, or plan a mini-fundraiser or collection with permission. Reflect on how the experience felt and what you learned about the world and yourself. Giving is not about being a hero; it's about being a neighbor.

Chapter 79 — Explore Careers

Careers are paths, not fixed boxes, and they often change as people learn new skills. Start by noticing what you enjoy doing for long stretches—solving puzzles, building things, performing, caring for others—and what environments energize you. Talk to adults about their work, ask what a typical day looks like, and learn which skills matter most. Clubs, electives, and short courses let you test interests in small, low- risk ways.

Create a simple list of strengths you can grow and questions you want to answer. Job shadowing or interviews can open doors you didn't know existed, and school projects can double as career experiments when you choose topics wisely. Keep your eyes on skills—communication,problem- solving, collaboration—because they travel with you across jobs. Your future isn't a single right answer; it's a set of options you prepare to explore.

Chapter 80 — Plan a Mini Event

Planning an event teaches teamwork, time, and budget in one joyful package. Start with a purpose—celebration, fundraiser, game night—and set a scale that fits your space and energy. Choose a date, a place, and a simple schedule, then make a list of supplies and roles. Invite people with clear details about time, location, and what to bring, and set up early so you can welcome guests with a smile.

During the event, pay attention to flow: greet newcomers, guide the group between activities, and solve small problems calmly. Keep receipts if you're handling money and clean up together so the space ends as nicely as it began. Afterward, thank helpers and write a short note about what worked and what to change next time. Each event you run becomes a rehearsal for bigger ideas you'll bring to life.

Communication & Creativity

Chapter 81 — Thank-You Notes

A thank-you note is a tiny gift that carries big warmth. Keep it simple and specific: name the person, name the gift or effort, and name the difference it made. Write soon so the moment stays bright in both your memories. Use a friendly greeting, one or two honest sentences about why you're grateful, and a natural sign-off. Spelling and neatness matter because they show care, but perfection is not required—sincerity is. Handwritten cards feel special; a clear email or message can be just as kind when sent thoughtfully.

Gratitude grows when you notice the hidden work behind help. Thank a coach not only for the trophy but for the extra practices; thank a friend not just for sharing notes but for helping you understand a tricky part. If you receive something you can't use, you can still thank the giver for thinking of you. Make a small habit of noticing kindness and speaking it out loud.

Chapter 82 — Email and Chat Etiquette

Messages travel farther than voices, so clarity and kindness matter. Begin emails with a short subject that says exactly what the message is about, add a polite greeting, and get to the point in a few calm sentences. Use paragraphs so ideas don't tangle, and close with a clear request or next step. In chats, match the tone to the space: classrooms and teams need complete thoughts, not fragments, and jokes that work with friends may not fit with teachers or new group members.

Respect people's time by reading before replying, checking attachments, and avoiding caps or punctuation that looks like shouting. Ask before adding people to group threads and be careful with tagging late at night or across time zones. If disagreements appear, cool down and choose words that solve the problem rather than winning the moment.

Chapter 83 — Tell a Short Story

A strong short story moves quickly from a character to a problem to a change. Start close to the action so the reader lands inside the moment, then show what your character wants and what stands in the way. Use concrete details your senses can catch—light on a hallway floor, the squeak of gym shoes, the taste of rain—to make the world feel real. Let dialogue sound like people actually speak, trimmed to the words that matter.

Every story breathes on structure: a beginning that hooks, a middle that tightens, and an end that reveals something new. After drafting, read aloud to hear where the rhythm stumbles and where a sentence can sharpen. Cut extra words, swap vague phrases for strong verbs, and check that the final lines land with meaning. The point is not magic twists; it is a small truth told clearly enough to live in someone else's head.

Chapter 84 — Give a Mini Talk

A memorable short talk starts with a single clear idea. Open with a simple hook—a question, a quick story, or a surprising fact—that pulls your audience in, then say your main point plainly. Offer a couple of examples that listeners can picture, and guide them toward a next step they can try today. Stand tall, breathe slowly, and look at real people rather than reading from your notes; your voice will follow your body's calm.

Practice is the secret. Run the talk out loud until your words feel like comfortable shoes, time it so you finish a little early, and imagine the space where you'll speak so your pacing fits. If nerves show up, treat them like extra energy you can steer. Afterward, ask one trusted person what was clear and what could tighten. A good talk is not about being flashy; it's about delivering help with care.

Chapter 85 — Creative Problem-Solving

Creativity begins with a well-framed question. Define the real problem, not just the first symptom, and collect a few constraints you must respect. Then let ideas flow without judging them too soon; wild thoughts often carry seeds you can shape into workable plans. When it's time to choose, look for solutions that are simple to test and kind to people who will live with the result. Small prototypes teach faster than long debates.

Reframing multiplies options. Ask what would happen if you removed a piece, swapped the order, or borrowed a method from a different field. Invite diverse voices to the table; new perspectives stretch what seems possible. After testing, keep what worked and learn from what failed, adjusting your approach with each round. Creative problem-solving is less about lightning bolts and more about steady, playful experiments that reveal the path forward.

Chapter 86 — Build from Instructions

Instructions are a conversation between a maker and a builder. Begin by reading the whole guide once so you know the shape of the journey, then check you have every part and tool the plan expects. Clear a workspace, organize pieces, and note step numbers so you can pause without losing your place. Work steadily, paying attention to orientation and order; most mistakes come from rushing a small detail that matters later.

When something doesn't fit, breathe, back up, and inspect rather than forcing it. Compare your build to diagrams, look for tiny markings, and consider whether a mirrored piece flipped the wrong way. Keep screws just snug until alignment looks true, then tighten. As you finish, test gently and make any final adjustments the instructions suggest. Building well teaches patience, precision, and pride in seeing an idea become something you can touch.

Chapter 87 — Drawing Basics

Drawing begins with seeing. Instead of naming objects—"a hand, a tree"—learn to notice shapes, angles, and the spaces between them. Lightly block in big forms, check proportions by holding out your pencil, and refine edges only after the structure feels right. Think in values as much as lines; shadows and highlights shape volume and make flat marks feel three-dimensional. Gesture sketches warm up your eyes and hands and keep drawings lively.

Tools are simple: paper that takes erasing, pencils of different softness, and an eraser used for lifting light as much as for fixing errors. Practice from life whenever you can and from photos when you must, and step back often to see the whole. Share your work with people who can offer specific feedback, and date your drawings so you can watch improvement accumulate. Drawing is not magic; it is attention made visible.

Chapter 88 — Music Practice

Progress in music comes from slow, focused work done often. Warm up your hands and voice, set a clear intention for the session, and practice small sections until they feel easy at a slow tempo. Use a metronome to build steady timing, but also listen for tone and phrasing so your playing sings, not just counts. Posture and relaxed hands protect your body and let sound travel freely.

Record short clips to hear what the room hears, and celebrate tiny wins—a cleaner shift, a smoother breath, a brighter chord. When a passage resists, change the rhythm, reverse the notes, or play only the skeleton of the phrase to reveal the trouble. End with a run-through that connects the parts into music again. Daily minutes beat occasional marathons, and patient practice becomes joy on stage.

Chapter 89 — Take Better Photos

Light is your main tool. Notice where it falls and how it shapes faces and objects, and move yourself rather than asking the sun to move. Early and late daylight is soft and warm, while mid-day can be harsh unless you find shade that diffuses brightness. Compose with intention: clear the background of distractions, place subjects where the frame supports the story, and try angles higher, lower, and closer until the picture feels alive.

Think in moments, not just poses. Be ready before something happens and shoot in short bursts so you catch the expression between words. Ask permission when appropriate and show respect for people and places. Edit lightly to match what you saw, organize images so you can find them later, and back them up so memories don't vanish. A good photo is a way of saying, "Look, this mattered."

Chapter 90 — Start a Journal

A journal is a safe place to think on paper. Date your entries, write a few honest lines about what happened and how it felt, and let your voice be plain rather than perfect. Mix forms as you like: lists of wins and worries, sketches, overheard sentences, questions for tomorrow. Some days you'll write more; some days a single sentence will be enough to keep the thread alive.

Privacy helps honesty, so set simple boundaries—where you keep the journal, who sees it—and respect others' notebooks the way you want yours respected. Over time you'll notice patterns: what energizes you, what drains you, which goals stick and which need reshaping. A journal is not homework; it is a conversation with your future self who will be glad you left a trail.

Technology & Media

Chapter 91 — Strong Passwords

Passwords protect your digital doors, and strong ones are long, unique, and hard to guess. A passphrase made of several unrelated words can be both memorable and strong, especially when you add numbers or symbols in ways only you would think of. Use a different password for each important account so one leak doesn't open many doors.

Add two-factor authentication when services offer it so a stolen password alone can't sign in. Be cautious of messages that try to trick you into sharing codes or clicking fake links, and keep your devices locked when unattended. Do not share passwords by message or note; if a guardian needs access, follow your family's plan for safe sharing. Good habits today protect future you.

Chapter 92 — Search Smart

Searching is more than typing a question; it is building a path to reliable answers. Start with a few strong keywords, then refine with quotation marks for exact phrases or symbols and filters that limit results by date or site. Skim several sources to compare facts and watch for agreement or useful disagreement, and note who created the information and why. Publication dates matter; newer isn't always better, but it often matters for fast- changing topics.

Evaluate credibility by checking an author's expertise, a site's reputation, and whether claims are supported with evidence you can trace. When stakes are high, cross- check with trusted references, librarians, or teachers who can point you to primary sources. Save or cite what you find so you can return to it, and keep your curiosity open. Smart searching turns the internet from a firehose into a helpful tap.

Chapter 93 — Balance Screen Time

Screens can teach, connect, and entertain, yet they can also crowd out sleep, movement, and face- to- face time. Create a simple plan with your family that matches your values: when and where screens are welcome, what content fits your age and goals, and which moments stay device- free so rest and relationships can breathe. Notice how different activities leave you feeling—energized, focused, or foggy—and adjust your habits toward what helps you thrive.

Build anchors that pull you off screens easily: a packed bag by the door for quick walks, a book on the table, a hobby that lives ready on your desk. Keep phones out of bedrooms at night when possible so sleep can do its work, and set gentle alarms for breaks during long sessions. Balance isn't about strict limits alone; it's about designing days where the best parts of life have room.

Chapter 94 — Respect Copyright

Creative work belongs to its creators. When you write, draw, film, or compose, you own your work; the same is true for others. Respect copyright by using your own creations, works you have permission to use, or materials in the public domain or shared under licenses that allow your kind of use. When you're learning about fair use or local exceptions, ask a teacher or librarian for guidance and remember that laws vary by place and situation.

Always credit sources clearly so people can find the original. If you're unsure whether you can use something, choose a different resource or ask for permission. Creating your own images, recordings, and text not only keeps you on the safe side of rules but also develops your skills. Respect for creators builds a culture where sharing is generous and honest.

Chapter 95 — Online Kindness

Kindness online is the same as kindness offline, only more important because tone can vanish in text. Before you post, pause and imagine your words arriving in someone else's day. Ask whether your message is true, necessary, and kind, and consider private conversations for sensitive topics. If you disagree, focus on ideas rather than people, and step away when tempers rise so you can return with a steady voice.

Be the kind of bystander who helps. If you see meanness, save evidence, report through the platform's tools, and check on the person targeted. Protect your privacy and others' by keeping personal details off public threads, and never share images or information without permission. Your digital trail becomes part of who you are; fill it with care, curiosity, and respect.

Chapter 96 — Back Up Your Work

Backups are promises to your future self. Devices fail, files corrupt, and accidents happen; a second copy turns a disaster into an inconvenience. Use a simple rule that fits your household—copies in more than one place, such as a cloud service and an external drive—and set automatic backups where possible so you don't have to remember. Label important versions clearly and store them in folders you can find later.

Test your backups occasionally by restoring a file to make sure your system works. Keep school projects and precious photos in the protected places from the start rather than shuffling them later. If your work includes private information, talk with a trusted adult about safe storage and account security. A good backup plan is invisible most days, then priceless the day you need it.

Chapter 97 — Coding Ideas

Coding is giving clear instructions to a computer and learning from what happens next. Start with tiny projects you can finish—drawing a shape, moving a character, sorting a list—and notice how variables, loops, and conditions let programs remember, repeat, and choose. When code misbehaves, read error messages like clues, print values to see inside the program, and change one thing at a time so you know what fixed the problem.

Write down what your program should do in plain language before you type, then translate that plan line by line. Share your projects, ask questions in friendly communities, and read other people's code to expand your toolbox. The best way to learn is to build something you want to use, then polish it. Coding rewards patience and curiosity; both grow each time you try.

Community & World

Chapter 98 — Be a Good Citizen

Citizenship is everyday care for the places you live, learn, and play. Follow the rules that keep people safe, return library books on time, sort trash the way your town asks, and show up for your community with respect. Stay informed from trustworthy local sources and talk about issues with curiosity instead of shouting. When you're old enough, civic duties like voting become part of your voice; until then, you still have many ways to contribute.

Good citizens notice needs and pitch in—holding doors, thanking public workers, or joining cleanups and drives that help neighbors. They speak up politely when something's wrong and listen when others speak. They remember that communities are built by many hands over many days.

Chapter 99 — Respect Differences

People differ in bodies, beliefs, languages, cultures, and ways of thinking, and those differences make groups stronger. Approach new experiences with curiosity rather than fear, ask questions respectfully, and listen for the stories behind choices you don't yet understand. Learn names and pronounce them with care. Use language that includes rather than excludes, and look for ways to make spaces accessible so more people can join.

When you notice a stereotype in your thoughts, pause and test it against real evidence; replace it with a more accurate view. If someone shares how a joke or habit harms them, believe them and adjust. Respect does not mean you must agree with everything; it means you grant others dignity while you explore your differences. The goal is not sameness—it is belonging.

Chapter 100 — Help the Planet

Planet care lives in daily choices and community action. Reduce waste by reusing what you can, repairing instead of replacing, and recycling according to your local rules. Save energy by turning off lights, unplugging idle chargers, and choosing to walk, bike, or share rides when it fits. Use water wisely by fixing drips, taking shorter showers, and watering plants during cooler hours. Small habits multiplied by many people change real numbers.

Learn about the ecosystems where you live and the species that share them, then help protect them through cleanups, planting native species, and supporting community efforts that improve air and water. Share what you learn with friends and family and listen for their ideas too. Caring for the planet is not about doing everything; it is about doing what you can, where you are, again and again.

Chapter 101 — Plan for the Future

Planning for the future is more about choosing a direction than locking in a destination. Think of a compass, not a cage. Your compass is made of values—kindness, curiosity, responsibility, courage—and the skills you're growing to live those values well. Picture the kind of person you want to become and the ways you hope to be useful. Set gentle horizons that you can actually reach: what you'll practice today, what you'll try this week, what you'll build this season. Write a one- line plan for each horizon and let habits carry the weight—read a little, move your body, sleep enough, manage your time, and save small amounts regularly. Systems like these keep you moving even when motivation is quiet.

Explore widely with small experiments. Join a club, shadow a job for a day, volunteer, start a tiny project, and pay attention to what feels meaningful and what doesn't. Keep a simple portfolio—notes, photos, links, and reflections—that shows what you've tried and what you learned. Ask mentors for stories about their paths and the skills that mattered most; thank them and report back on your progress. Protect your options by caring for your health, treating people well, backing up your work, and tending your digital footprint with respect. Review your plans every few months: keep what works, adjust what doesn't, and trade perfect plans for adaptable ones when life changes. When you stumble, treat failure as data and try again with a smarter step. The future is built by many ordinary days of learning, building, and serving. Keep your compass steady, take the next right step, and let time turn your small actions into a life that fits you—and helps others, too.